THE PEOP

SKENE

&

KINELLAR

1696

taken from
List of Pollable Persons in the Shires of Aberdeen
1696

Volume 2

The Book or List off Poleable persons
within the Shire off **Aberdein** & Burghs
within the same

Containing the names off the haill persons
poleable and Polemoney payable, be them
Conforme to their respective capacities According
to the Act off Parliament anent Polemoney
daited the   day of

Faithfullie extracted ffurth of the Princip. all
Lists off poleable persons off each paroch within y.
Shyre, as they were reported by the Commission.
and Clerks for the severall paroches appointed —
ffor that effect

By *William Hay* Collector appointed off
the polemoney peyable ffurth of the said shire

And revised and examined by ane Quorum
of the **Commissioners** of Supplie off the
Samen Shyre and attested by them :
                              ffirst day of Aprile 1696.

This Book belongs to
Thomas Gordon of Buthlaw

INTRODUCTION

During the late seventeenth century the Scottish economy cupboard was bare and the need for extra revenue was essential. One of the ways used was a tax on people- A POLL TAX - and several were collected during the 1690's. Supposedly a tax on every person over the age of sixteen not a beggar,although this has been disputed. Therefore for genealogical purposes an extant list of over 30,000 names from 1696 is of immense value. Even more so is the transcription and publication,in two volumes, of this unique document by the Gentlemen of the County in 1844. It is from this edition that our facsimile reprint comes,also included is two pages from the original 1696 volume.

Anyone wishing to check the original will find it in Aberdeen University Archives (MS548). Our thanks must go to the staff of both the Archives and Special Collections departments of the University Library for their help. The two photographs of the original are reproduced by kind permission of the Archives.Although dated 1696 the date the lists were approved, in fact they were compiled in September 1695.

A history of the original volume is also interesting - it was in the library of Thomas Gordon of Buthlaw and his descendants till their fortunes failed and the estate was sold during the First World War. The book was then bought by Col. D.F.Davidson who donated it to Aberdeen University in the 1920's.

In the Special Collections department of the University (housed in the same building as the Archives) there exists an Index to the 'List' compiled in the 19th century by Dingwall Fordyce,however it is a very selective list consisting only of the more 'important' people. The index included here is comprehensive and also includes a place name index as well as an occupation breakdown.

Several points have to be made to make understanding this volume easier:
1) Any errors in the 1844 published version have been perpetuated in this edition.
2) The original page numbers of the 1844 edition have been used throughout.
3) The following places have not been located on the maps - ATHRENCROFT, CAIRNSLUM,CARNOUSTIE,MILNBOGG,WOODEND.

LESLEY DIACK.

MALES 329
FEMALES 294
UNSPECIFIED 2

TOTAL 625

ANE LIST of the POLLABLE PERSONS within the PAROCHIN of SKIN, given up be the LAIRD *of [   ], and* ANDREW BURNETT *in Blackhiles, two Commissioners appoyntet for that effect, and be* JAMES STIVEN, *Clerk and Colecter chosen be them.*

THE VALOVATON of the haill pariochen of Skine is...................£2500 6 &

The EARLE of KINTOIR his valovatone in the said pariochin is................. £170 0 0

The howndreth pairt whereof payable by the tennents is............................. £1 14 0
 John Keith, for the lands of Auchinclech, his proportione of the valowaton
  is £0 8 6
 James Fouler ther, his proportion is.................................... 0 8 6
 John Forbes, tennent in Bothomfawld, is........................... 0 8 6
 John Aitken, tennent in Milne of Brisok, is......................... 0 8 6
                  —————— 1 14 0

AUCHINCLECH.
John Keith, posessor of Auchinclech, of valowaton is 8s. 6d., but lyabell not in
 poll, he having classed himself as ane heritor, paying £4 of poll, he
 being feftie pownds of valued rent, with 6s. of generall poll, is......... £4 6 0
Item, James Keith, his son *in familia,* his generall poll is.......................... 0 6 0
Item, William Menie, his servant, hes of fee per annum £9, the fortieth part
 whereof and generall poll is... 0 10 6
Item, Elizabeth Caddell, his servant, of fee per annum £6, including bounties,
 the fortieth pairt whereof and generall poll is.............................. 0 9 0
Item, Robert Ross, herd, of fee per annum £2, the fortieth pairt whereof and
 generall poll is... 0 7 0
Item, Alexander Sharp, and Robert Forbes, cottars, and their wives, poll is...... 1 4 0
Item, Agnes Miln, grasswoman, her generall poll..................................... 0 6 0
JAMES FOWLER ther, his proportione of his walowation is 8s. 6d., and with his
 own and his wyfes generall poll... 1 0 6
Item, Margrat Fowler, his daughter *in familia,* her generall poll.................... 0 6 0
Item, Georg Fraser, his servant, his fee per annum £8, the fortieth pairt where-
 of and generall poll is... 0 10 0

Item, William Davedson, cordoner, for his trad 6s., with 6s. for his own and his
wifes generall poll, is.. £0 18 0
Item, William Chalmers, cottar, and his own and his wyfes generall poll is...... 0 12 0
Item, Elspet Fowler, Margrat Wallers, and Agnes Wilson, their generall
poll is... 0 18 0
Item, Wiliam Fouler, his generall poll is.. 0 6 0
Item, Alexander Bowie, his servant, of fee £2, the fortieth pairt whereof and
generall poll is... 0 7 0
Item, James Gray ther, his generall poll is... 0 6 0

£12 12 0

BODDOMFAWLD.
John Forbes, tennent ther, his proportione of the walowatone is 8s. 6d., with
his own and his wyfes generall poll is.................................... £1 6 0
Item, Bess Brothwall, his servand, of fee per annum £4, the fortieth pairt
whereof and generall poll is... 0 8 0
Item, Alexander Clark, cottar ther, and his wyfe, their generall poll is........... 0 12 0
Item, William Bothwall, cottar ther, and his wyfe, their generall poll is......... 0 12 0
Item, William Shirres, and his wyfe, their generall poll is........................... 0 12 0

£3 4 6

BRISSOCK.
John Aitkine, tennent ther, his proportione of the walovatone 8s. 6d., the fortieth
pairt whereof with the generall poll is.................................... £0 14 6
Item, his wyfe of generall poll is.. 0 6 0
Item, William Keith, his servant, of fee per annum £10, the fortieth pairt
whereof and generall poll is... 0 11 0
Item, Katren Donald, his servant, of fee per annum £6, the fortieth pairt wher-
of and generall poll is.. 0 9 0
Item, Katren Johnston, servant (no fee), her generall poll is....................... 0 6 0
Item, John Clark, hird, of fee per annum £2, the fortieth pairt wherof and ge-
nerall poll is... 0 7 0
James Mitchell, miller at Brissocks Mile, for his tred 6s., and his wyfes and his
own generall poll, is.. 0 18 0
Item, Thomas Clark, subtennent, for his wyfes and his own generall poll is...... 0 12 0
Item, John Strayhen, subtennent, for his own and his wyfe their generall poll is 0 12 0
Item, John Broun, vywer, for his tread 6s., with his owen and his wyfes gene-
rall poll is.. 0 18 0
Item, John Craigheid, talyor, for his tred 6s., with his own and his wyfes gene-
rall poll.. 0 18 0
Item, James Dawedson, cordoner, for his tred 6s., his owen and his wyfes generall poll... 0 18 0

£7 9 6

*A List of the Pollable Persones within the Pariochen of Skein, Tennents and others in Fornet,
belonging also to the* EARELL *of* KINTOR, *with their proportones of the valovat rent.*

The valuatioue of the LANDS of FORNET is yearly................................... £290 0 0

The houndreth pairt whereof, payable be the tennents, is.............................. £2 18   0

Imprimis, James Chessor, tennent in Fornat, his owen and his wyfes generall
    poll is... 0 12   0
Item, Hellen Chessor, his daughter *in familia*, of generall poll is.................. 0   6   0
Item, Alexander Crombie, servant, of fee per annum £12, the fortieth pairt
    whereof and generall poll is.. 0 12   0
Item, Georg Stiven and Patrick Walker, subtennents, and their wyfes, poll is... 1   4   0
Item, William Gordon, subtennent ther, his owen and his wyfes poll is........... 0 12   0
Item, THOMAS JAMESON, tennent ther, his own and his wyfes generall poll is... 0 12   0
Item, William Loggan, his servand, of fee per annum is £12, the fortieth pairt
    whereof and generall poll is.. 0 12   0
Item, Janet Walker, servant, of fee per annum £6, the fortieth pairt whereof
    and generall poll is... 0   9   0
Item, Daved Shirres, subtennent ther, his own and his wyfes generall poll is.... 0 12   0
Item, Robert Barron, subtennent ther, his own and his wyfes generall poll is... 0 12   0

                                                              £6 3 0

FORNETT.

John Williamson, tennent, for his own and his wyfes generall poll is............. £0 12   0
Item, James Nose, his servant, of fee per annum £8, the fortieth pairt where-
    of and generall poll is... 0 10   0
Item, Janet Duncan, servant, of fee per annum £2, the fortieth pairt whereof
    and generall poll is.. 0   7   0
Item, John Alerdes, herd, of fee per annum £2, the fortieth pairt whereof and
    generall poll is 0   7   0
Item, William Davedson, subtennent ther, and his wife, their generall poll is 0 12   0
Item, William Johnston, subtennent ther, and his wife, ther generall poll is.... 0 12   0
Item, John Frost, cottar ther, his own generall poll, with his wifes, is............. 0 12   0

                                                              £3 12 0

WALKER PLEUGH OF FORNETT.

Alexander Melvell, subtennent ther, his generall poll, and his wyfes, is......... £0 12   0
Item, Alexander Frost, cottar ther, his generall poll, and his wyfes, is............ 0 12   0
Item, Gilbert Talyor, cottar ther, and his wyfe, their generall poll is............... 0 12   0
Item, Georg Biddie and James Watt ther, their own and their wyfes poll is.... 1   4   0

                                                              £3 0 0

The HEAIRS of CREAIGMYLL their waloed rent in the pariochen of Skein amonts
    to £1340 0 0

The hundereth pairt whereof, payable be the tennents....... .... £13 8   0

Item, Robert Fraser, tennent, his proportion of the valovation
    for Kinmondie is... £0   9   0
John Milne, tennent in Kinmondi, is..................................... 0   5   4
Peter Duncan, tennent ther, his proportion is......................... 0   5   4
Androw Duncan, tennent in Blackhills................................ 0   6   6

Julian Keith, tennent in Ord, is..	£1	1	8
Gilbert Smith, tennent in Ord, his proportion........................	0	10	0
John Farnie, tennent ther, is..	0	0	6
Androw Smith, tennent in Easter Kerney, is...........................	0	7	6
Alexander Reiry, tennent ther, is...	0	7	6
William Leith, tennent in Ister Kerny, is.........	0	3	9
Alexander Dollas, in Ester Kairney, is.................................	0	3	9
Alexander Smith, in Wester Carney.....................................	0	8	0
Patrik Smith, tennent in Waster Kernie...............................	0	8	0
John Smith, tennent in Waster Kernie, is..............................	0	8	0
Arthur Morris in Waster Carneye	0	6	0
Alexander Crombie, tennent in Garlogie, is	0	7	0
Robert Walker, tennent in Garlogie, is	0	1	11
Androw Deuchars, tennent in Garlogie, is.............................	1	5	6
George Leith, tennent in Fidde, his proportione	0	4	4
William Murdo, tennent in Fiddie, his proportione..................	0	4	4
James Smith, tennent in Milbuie, is.....................................	0	7	5
Gilbert Dun, tennent in Milbuie	0	7	5
George Melvell, tennent in Milbuie, is	0	7	5
William Norij, tennent in Rodgerhill, is	0	6	6
William Ronaldson, tennent in Kirkton, is	0	9	11
Androw Louson, tennent in Kirkton, is	0	9	11
George Reid, tennent in Kirkton, is.....................................	0	8	5
Thomas Davedson, tennent ther, his proportione is.................	0	5	9
Daved Talzor, tennent ther, his proportione is	0	0	10
Alexander Shirres, tennent ther, his proportione is.................	0	0	6
James Booth, tennent ther, his proportione is	0	0	8
Alexander Fergus, tennent ther, his proportione is..................	0	1	11
Margrat Snowie, tennent ther, her proportione is	0	1	11
Alexander Snowie, tennent ther, his proportione is.................	0	0	8
James Reid, tennent in Kirkton, his proportione is..................	0	3	6
James Snovie ther, tennent, his proportione is.......................	0	1	6
Donald Then, tennent in Kirktoun, is...................................	0	1	6
Alexander Nicoll, tennent ther, is	0	1	6
William Strayhen, tennent ther, is.......................................	0	0	9
William Strachan, minor, tennent ther, is	0	0	9
John Duff, tennent in Hill of Kirktone, is.............................	0	5	11
George Mill, tennent in Liddoch, is.....................................	0	6	7
Alexander Norie, tennent ther, is..	0	5	6
John Rid, tennent in Brodiach, is..	0	2	8
James Rane, tennent in Eister Carni, is	0	7	6
John Davedson, tennent in Lidach, is	0	5	6
	£13	8	0

WAST CREIG.

Patrick Smith, tennent, his oven and his wifes generall poll.........................	£0	12	0
Item, for his freie stok of 600 merks	2	10	0

3 Q

Item, John Masone, his servant, whose fee £20, fortieth part and generall poll, £0 12 8
Item, Agnes Hendry, his servant, of fee £8, the fortieth part and generall poll, 0 10 0
Item, John Milne, herd, fee including bwntis £4, fortieth part and generall poll, 0 8 0
Item, Robert Henderson, herd, of fee £2, fortieth part and generall poll is...... 0 7 0
Item, James Mill, subtennent, and his wife, of generall poll is 0 12 0
Item, John Rae, subtennent, and [his wife], and Bessie Talzor, grasswyfe, poll, 0 18 0

£6 9 8

LIDDACH.

George Milne, tennent ther, his proportione of the valovation is 6s. 3d., and
    his own and his wifes generall poll is.. £0 18 3
Item, Gilbert Smith, his son in law *in familia*, his generall poll..................... 0 6 0
Item, Elizabeth Low, his servant, of fee £4, the fortieth part and generall poll, 0 8 0
Item, William Robertson, herd, of fee £2, the fortieth part and generall poll... 0 7 0
Item, Robert Shirres, Robert Gall, and John Then, subtennents, and ther wives, 1 16 0
Item, William Walker, talzor, for his trade 6s., his own and his wifes poll, is... 0 18 0
John Aberdein, wyver ther, for his trade 6s., with his own and his wifes poll, is 0 18 0
Item, Robert Aberdine, his son *in familia*, his generall poll........................... 0 6 0
Item, Thomas Beverlay, subtennent, his own and wifes generall poll............... 0 12 0
Item, Margrat and Issobell Beverlys, his daughters *in familia*, their poll is...... 0 12 0
Item, Alexander Stephen, cottar, his own and his wifes generall poll is........... 0 12 0

£7 13 3

GARLOGIE.

Item, Robert Walker, walker at the Milne of Garlogie, his proportion of the va-
    lovatione 1s. 11d., with 6s. for his trade, and 6s. for his ovn, and 6s.
    for his sons generall poll *in familia*, is... £0 19 11
Item, Margrat Then, his servant, of fee £6, the fortieth [pairt] and generall poll, 0 9 0
Item, Robert Syme, his servant (no fee), of generall poll is......................... 0 6 0

£1 14 11

EISTER CARNEY.

James Raney, tennent in Eester Kerney, his proportion of the valawatione
    is 7s. 6d., with his owen and his wyfes generall poll is £0 19 6
Item, John Sharp, his servant, of fee per annum £8, the fortieth pairt whereof,
    with the generall poll, is 0 10 0
Item, Agnes Cowper, his servant, of fee per annum £4, the fortieth pairt where-
    of and generall poll is 0 8 0
Item, John Adam, herd, the lyk fee and generall poll is 0 8 0
Item, George Clark, cordner ther, 6s. for his trade, 6s. for his ovn, and 6s. for
    his wyfes generall poll is.. ... 0 18 0
Item, George Strayhen, cottar ther, and his wyfe, generall poll is................. 0 12 0
ALEXANDER RANEY ther, his proportione of the valowation is 7s. 6d., with his
    ovn and his wyfes generall poll is 0 19 6
Item, James Watt, his servant, per annum of fee £18, the fortieth pairt where-
    of and generall poll is 0 10 0
Item, James Irving, herd, £3 of fee per annum, fortieth pairt and generall poll, 0 7 6
Item, James Booth, subtennent and smith, for his trade, his ovn and his wyfes
    generall poll is 0 18 0

Item, John Booth, his son *in familia*, his generall poll is.............................. £0 6 0
Item, Robert Low, wyver, for his trade 6s., and his own and his wyfes ge-
nerall poll is 0 18 0
Item, John Ranei ther, his generall poll is.. 0 6 0

£8 0 6

FIDDIE.
George Leith, tennent in Fiddie, his proportion of the walovation is 4s. 4d.,
with his ovn and his wyfes generall poll is £0 16 4
Item, Alexander Robe, his servant, of fee per annum is £8, the fortieth pairt
whereof and generall poll is 0 10 0
Item, Elizabath Sharp and Elisabath Bisset, grasswomen, ther generall poll is 0 12 0
Item, William Bisset, grassman, [his] generall poll is 0 6 0

£2 4 4

HILL OF KEIR.
John Duff, tennent ther, his proportion of the valovatione is 5s. 11d., with his
ovne and his wyfes, generall poll is... £0 17 11
Item, John Robe, his servant, fee £8, the fortieth pairt and generall poll 0 10 0
Item, Margrat Beaine, his servant, fee £8, fortieth pairt and generall poll is ... 0 10 0
Item, James Clark, herd, fee £4, fortieth pairt and generall poll.................. 0 8 0
Item, William Bisset, herd, fee £3, the fortieth pairt and generall poll 0 7 6
Item, John Burlay, subtennent ther, his own and his wyfes generall poll is...... 0 12 0
Item, Robert Davedson, swbtennent ther, his ovn and daughters generall poll, 0 12 0
Item, Alexander Duncan, subtennent, for his oven and his wyfes generall poll, 0 12 0

£4 9 5

MILBUIE.
George Melvell, tennent ther, his proportion of the valovatione is 7s. 5d., with
his wyfes and his own generall poll is £0 19 5
Item, Walter Clark, servant, fee £18, the fortieth pairt and generall poll is 0 15 0
Item, Marjorie Low, servant, fee £8, the fortieth pairt and generall poll is 0 10 0
Item, John Gray, herd, fee £5, the fortieth pairt whereof and generall poll is... 0 8 6
Item, Thomas Peterson and George Clark, herds, fee £2 10s., the fortieth pairt
and generall poll is.. 0 14 4
Item, Alexander Berii, sivvright, for his trade 6s., with his oven and his wyfes
generall poll, is 0 18 0
John Berii, his son *in familia*, of generall poll 0 6 0
Thomas Melvell, swbtennent, his generall [poll] and his wyfes is.................. 0 12 0
Item, Patrick Cruickshank, subtennent, his generall poll and his wyfes is....... 0 12 0
John Clark, cordnar, for his trade 6s., his ovn and his wyfes generall poll is ... 0 18 0
Item, Alexander Crombie, vnmeryed, his generall poll is 0 12 0
Item, Ana Irving, grasswoman, her generall poll is 0 6 0

£7 11 3

EIST KINMUNDY.
John Milln, tennent ther, his proportion of the valovatione is 5s. 4d., with his
ovn and his wyfes generall poll is £0 17 4
Item, Jane Wilson, servant, of fee per annum £5, the fortieth part whereof with
the generall poll is.. 0 8 6

Item, [   ] Bowman, herd, his fee £4 10s., the fortieth part and generall poll, £0   8   2
Item, Alexander Straghen, wyver, for his trade 6s., and 6s. of his ovn and his
    wyfes generall poll is 0 18   0
Item, Agnes Straghen, his daughter *in familia*, her generall poll is................ 0   6   0
PATRICK DWNCAN, tennent ther, his proportione of the valowatione is 5s. 4d.,
    and his ovn and his wyfes generall poll is 0 17   4
Item, Issobell Stephen, of fee per annum £6, the fortieth part with her poll is... 0   9   0
Item, George Caddell, subtennent ther, for his own, his wyfe, and his daughter,
    Margrat *in familia*, their generall poll is 0 18   0
John Hunter and Alexander Gabriell, subtennents, and their wyves, poll is...... 1   4   0

                                                      £6   6   4

KERKTOUNE.

George Reid, tennent ther, his proportione of the valowatione is 8s. 5d., with his
    own and his wyfes, and and sone *in familia*, their generall poll is £1   6   5
Item, Alexander Allerdys, subtennent, of generall poll for himself and wyfe is 0 12   0
Item, Issebell Low, grasswyfe, of generall poll is............................. 0   6   0
Item, Androw Philpe, grassman, and his wyfe, their generall poll is.............. 0 12   0

                                                      £2 16   5

WEST CARNEY.

John Smith, tennent ther, his proportione of the valowatione is 8s., with his own
    generall poll and his wyfes is £1   1   0
Item, James Machrey, his servant, of fee £16, the fortieth part and generall poll, 0 14   0
Item, Agnes Fraser, his servant, of fee £6, the fortieth part and generall poll is 0   9   0
James Reid, herd, of fee per annum £4, the fortieth part and and generall poll, 0   8   0
William Straghen, subtennent ther, and cordiner, 6s. for his trade, with his own
    and his wyfes generall poll is 0 18   0
Item, Gilbert Wabster, subtennent ther, his own and his wyfes generall poll is 0 12   0
Item, Alaster Reid, subtennent ther, his ovn and his wyfes generall poll is 0 12   0
Item, Janett [   ] ther, her generall poll... 0   6   0

                                                      £4 19   0

EIST CARNEY.

Androw Smith, tennent ther, his proportione of the valowed rent is 7s. 6d., with
    the generall poll for himself and wyfe is..................................... £0 19   6
Item, George Shirres, his servant, of fee £16, the fortieth part with generall poll, 0 14   0
Item, Helen Bodwall, servant, of fee £6, the fortieth part with generall poll is 0   9   0
Item, James Garro, herd, of fee per annum £4, fortieth part with generall poll, 0   8   0
Item, John Gallow, subtennent, and his wyfe, their generall poll is.................. 0 12   0
Alexander Low, wright, for his trade 6s., with his own and his wifes poll is 0 18   0
Item, James Low, his son *in familia*, of generall poll.................................. 0   6   0
Item, Margrat Galo ther, her generall poll is.. 0   6   0
Item, the said Androw Smith, of poll for his free esteat, given vp abowt 500 or
    600 merks, is.. 2 10   0

                                                      £7   2   6

MILNBUIE.

Gilbert Dun, tennent ther, his proportione of the walovatione is 7s. 5d., with the
    generall poll 6s. for himself, and 6s. for his wyfe is...................... £0 19   5

Item, John [   ], his servant of fee £16, the fortieth part and generall poll is £0 14 0
Item, John Millne, herd, of fee £4, the fortieth part whereof and generall poll, 0 8 0
Item, Janet Simson, servant, of fee £6, the fortieth pairt and generall poll is... 0 9 0
Item, Margrat Philp, servant, of fee £3 6s. 8d. per annum, the fortieth part and
  generall poll is 0 7 1
Item, James Philp, of fee as herd £2, the fortieth part and generall poll is...... 0 7 0
Item, John Stiphen and George Miln, subtennents, and their wives, poll is...... 1 4 0
Item, the said Gilbert Dun is lyable for his stock, being abovt 500 or 600 merks, 2 10 0

                  £6 18 6

GARLOGIE.

Androw Deuchers, tennent ther, his proportion of the valowation is £1 5s. 6d.,
  [with] his ovn and his wyfes poll generall is............................... £1 17 5
Item, John Mackie, his seruant, of fee per annum £16 13s. 4d., the fortieth
  part whereof and generall poll is.. .. 0 14 4
Item, Isobell Low, servant, of fee per annum £6, the fortieth pairt and poll is 0 9 0
Item, John Killo, herd, of fee £4 per annum, the fortieth part whereof and
  generall poll is 0 8 0
Item, William [   ], herd, of fee £2 per annum, the fortieth pairt whereof
  and generall poll is.. 0 7 0
Item, John Hall, subtennent ther, for his ovn and wyfes generall poll........... 0 12 0
Item, Androw Miln, subtennent ther, his wife, and Margrat Milne, [their]
  daughter, poll is.. 0 18 0
Item, Alexander Low, wyver, for his trad 6s. with his ovn and his wifes poll is 0 18 0
Item, John Wagrall, subtennent, and his wyfe, of generall poll is.................. 0 12 0
Item, Margrat Gall ther, her generall poll is................................... 0 6 0
Item, Alexander Reid, milner, for his trade 6s., with his oven, and his wyfe,
  and William Reid, his son *in familia*, generall poll is.................... 1 4 0

                  £8 5 9

KERKTOUNE.

Andrew Lousone, tennent ther, his proportione of the valovaton is 9s. 11d., with
  his own and his wyfes generall poll is..................................... £1 1 11
Item, William Davedson, servant, of fee £16, fortieth part and generall poll... 0 14 0
Item, William Louson, herd, of fee £2, the fortieth part and generall poll...... 0 7 0
Item, John Norrie, subtennent, and his wyfe, of generall poll is.................... 0 12 0
Item, Daved Talzor, wyver ther, for his trade 6s., and generall poll for himself
  and wyfe, and John Taylor, his son *in familia*, is......................... 1 4 0

                  £3 18 11

FIDDIE.

William Murdo, tennent ther, his proportion of the valovation is 4s. 4d., with
  his own, his wife, and George Murdo, his son, generall poll is......... £1 2 4
Item, Margrat Murdo, his daughter *in familia*, generall poll.................... 0 6 0
Item, James Gall, and Robert Rid, subtennents, and their wives, poll is......... 1 4 0

                  £2 12 4

ORD.

Gilbert Smith in Ord, his proportione of the walowaton is 10s., with his own and
  his wifes generall poll is... £1 2 0

Item, James Chalmers, servant, of fee £16, fortieth pairt and generall poll is... £0 14 0
Item, Margrat Spring, servant, fee £6, the fortieth part and generall poll is... 0 9 0
Item, Isobell Selvie, servant, and James Kilgour, herd, lyk fee and poll each... 0 18 0
Item, Thomas Marre, and Alexander Forbes, subtennents, and their wives, poll, 1 4 0
Item, Dawed Creaig, wyver, for his trade 6s., with his own and his wifes poll is 0 18 0
Item, John Farnie, subtennent, and his wife, of generall poll...................... 0 12 0

£5 17 0

KIRKTOUNE.

James Reid, tennent in Kirktoune, his proportion of the valowatone is 3s. 6d.,
    with his own and wyfes generall poll is.................................... £0 15 6
James Snovie, wyver, his proportion of the walowation is 1s. 6d., with his own
    and his wifes generall poll, with 6s. for his trade, is........................ 0 19 6
Item, Margrat Snowie ther, for generall poll and proportion of the valowaton is 0 7 1
Item, Issobell Bean, servant, of fee £6, fortieth pairt and generall poll is...... 0 9 0
Item, William Straqn, cordner, for his trade 6s., with his own and his wifes
    generall poll, and his proportion of the valovatone is..................... 1 7 0
Item, Alexander Snowi, wyver, and tennent in Kerkton, his proportion of the
    walovation is 8d., with 6s. for his trade, his own and his wifes poll is 0 18 8
Item, Alexander Philp, servant (no fee), his generall poll is........................ 0 6 0
Item, ALEXANDER SHIRRES, tennent ther, his proportion of the walovation 6d.,
    with his own and wyfes generall poll is..................................... 0 12 6
Item, Walter Innes ther, and his wyfe, of generall poll is............................ 0 12 0
DONALD THAIN, tennent in Kerkton, his proportion of walovation 1s. 6d, [with]
    his own, his wife, and Margrat Then, his daughter, generall poll is... 0 19 6
Item, Issobell Hay, recidenter ther, her generall poll is............................ 0 6 0
John Robertson, talzor, for his trade 6s., with 6s. of poll for himself and wife, is 0 18 0
Item, Margrat Rowan ther, of generall poll is..................................... 0 6 0
Item, ALEXANDER NICOLL, tennent in Kerktone, his proportion of the walovaton
    is 1s. 6d., with his own and wyfes generall poll is........................ 0 13 6
William Straghen, minor, tennent and talzor, his proportione of the valowation
    is 9d., with 6s. of poll for his trade, with his own and his wyfes poll, is 0 18 9
Item, Cristan Turner ther, her generall poll is..................................... 0 6 0
Item, Issobell Moir ther, and Issobell and Jane Lowes, her daughters, poll is... 0 18 0
Item, George Dovnie ther, for himself and wyfe, generall poll..................... 0 12 0
Item, JAMES BOOTH ther, tennent, his proportione of the walovation is 8d.,
    with his wyfes and his own generall poll..................................... 0 12 8
Item, Elizabeth Gearioch ther, her generall poll is.................................... 0 6 0
THOMAS DAVEDSON, tennent ther, his proportione of the valovatione is 5s. 9d.,
    with his own and his wyfes generall poll is.................................. 0 17 9
Item, ALEXANDER FERGUS, tennent ther, his proportione of the valovatione is
    1s. 11d. [with] his wyfe and his own generall poll is....................... 0 13 11
Item, Elspet Elmslie, his servant, fee £6, fortieth pairt and generall poll........ 0 9 0
Item, Janet Sheires, his servant, the lyk fee and generall poll..................... 0 9 0
Item, WILLIAM RONALDSON ther, tennent, his proportion of the valovatione [is]
    9[s.] 11d., [with] his own and his wyfes generall poll, is.................. 1 1 11
Item, John Talzor, his servant, fee £16, fortieth pairt and generall poll........... 0 14 0

Item, Alexander Murray, subtennent, for himself and wyfe of generall poll is... £0 12 0
Item, Alexander Wagrall, herd, fee £2, the fortieth pairt and generall poll is... 0 7 0
ALEXANDER CROMBIE, tennent ther, his proportione of the valovatione is 7s. 8d.,
    with his oun and his wyfes generall poll is.................................... 0 19 8
Item, James Wobster, his servant, fee £8, fortieth pairt and generall poll is... 0 10 0
Item, Issobell Thom, servant, fee £4, [fortieth pairt] and generall poll is......... 0 8 0
Item, John Killo, subtennent, for himself and wyfe, their generall poll is......... 0 12 0
Item, Margrat Robertson, grassvoman ther, of generall poll is...................... 0 6 0

            £21 3 11

BLACKHILL.

Androw Burnet, tennent ther, his proportione of the valovatione is 6s. 6d., with
    his oun, his wyfes, and Thomas Burnet, his son *in familia*, their poll is £1 4 6
Item, Margrat Mackie, her generall poll is... 0 6 0
Item, Alexander Strayhen, servant, fee £12, fortieth pairt and generall poll is... 0 12 0
Item, Elizabeth Thomsone, fee £6, fortieth pairt and generall poll is.............. 0 9 0
Item, William Straghen, subtennent, for' himself and wyfe, their generall poll is 0 12 0
Item, George Mill and William Gray, subtennents, and their wyfes, poll is...... 1 4 0
Item, Alexander Reid, vyver ther, for his trade 6s., with his oun, his wyfe, and
    his sones generall poll.. 1 4 0
Item, John Lyg, subtennent ther, his generall poll, and the generall poll of 6s.
    for Janet Stump... 0 12 0

            £6 3 6

LIDDOCH.

John Davedson, tennent ther, his proportion of his masters valovation is 5s. 6d.,
    with his oun and his wyfe generall poll, is................................... £0 17 6
Item, James Leith, his servant, fee £8, fortieth pairt and generall poll is......... 0 10 0
Item, Ana Wilhows, servant, of fee £6, fortieth pairt and generall poll.......... 0 9 0
Item, John Davidson, elder, subtennent, for himself and wyfes generall poll.... 0 12 0
Item, John Chalmer, subtennent ther, for himself and his wyfe of generall poll, 0 12 0
ALEXANDER NORRIE, tennent ther, his proportione of tho walovation is 5s. 6d.,
    with his oun, his wyfe, and Alexander, his sons generall poll............ 1 3 6
Item, Elizabeth Findlay, servant, fee £6, fortieth pairt and generall poll is...... 0 9 0
Item, Alexander Walker, wyver ther, for himself and his wyfe, poll............... 0 18 0
Item, John Walker, subtennent, for himself [and his wyfe] and generall poll... 0 12 0
Item, Margrat Henderson, grasswoman ther, her generall poll is.................... 0 6 0

            £6 19 0

ORD.

Julian Kith, tennent ther, his proportione of his masters valovation is £1 1s.,
    with his own generall poll is £1 7 8
Item, Robert Strachen, servant, of fee £12, fortieth pairt and generall poll is, 0 12 0
Item, Issobell Forbes, servant, of fee 14 merks, fortieth pairt and generall poll, 0 10 8
Item, Margrat Talzor, servant, of fee £2, the fortieth part and generall poll is... 0 7 0

            £2 17 4

GRAYSTONE.

Alexander Dollas, tennent ther, his proportione of his masters valoved rent be-
    ing 3s. 9d., with the generall poll of himself and his wife, is £0 15 9

Item, William Leith, Alexander Gallo, and William King, subtennents, and their wives, generall poll is.. 1 16 0

£2 11 9

RODGERHILL.

William Norrie, tennent ther, his proportione of his masters valowatione is 6s. 6d., with his ovn and his wifes generall poll, is £0 18 6

Item, William Norrie, his son *in familia*, his generall poll is......................... 0 6 0

Item, James Bisset and James Adam, subtennents, and their wives, their poll, 1 4 0

£2 8 6

BROODIACH.

John Reid, tennent ther, his proportion of the valovatione is 2s. 8d., and for his trade as skinner 6s., with his own and his wifes generall poll, is £1 0 8

MILBUIE.

James Smith in Milbuie, tennent, his proportione of his masters valloyatione is 7s. 5d., with his ovn, and his wifes, and his childring, viz., Thomas and Janet Smith, his childring *in familia*, of generall poll, *inde*......... £1 11 5

Item, Alexander Hall, his servant, of fee £8, fortieth pairt and generall poll, 0 10 0

Item, John Watt, servant, of fee £3, fortieth pairt and generall poll is............ 0 7 6

Item, John Devenie, his servant, of lyk fee, with generall poll, is................... 0 7 6

£3 17 1

Subtennents.

Item, James Greig and his wyfe, of generall poll is..................................... £0 12 0

Item, Agnes Thomson, grasswoman ther, her generall poll is....................... 0 6 0

Item, John Murey, subtennent ther, his own and his wyfes generall poll is 0 12 0

Item, Patrek Snawie, wyver, for his trade 6s., with his own and his wyfes poll, 0 18 0

Item, Robert Hownter, subtennent, his own and his wyfes generall poll is 0 12 0

£3 0 0

KINMONDY.

Robert Fraser, tennent ther, his proportione of the valowatione is 9s. 8d., with his own and his wyfes generall poll is.................................... 1 1 8

Item, Thomas and Issobell Frasers, his childring, poll ilk ane 6s.................. 0 12 0

John Faenie, servant, of fee £6, the fortieth part whereof and generall poll is... 0 9 0

Euphen Allan, servant, of fee £6, the fortieth part whereof and generall poll is 0 9 0

Item, Alexander Galow, servant, for fee £2, the fortieth part and generall poll, 0 7 0

Item, Alexander Leith and James Ros, subtennents and their wyves, their poll, 1 4 0

Item, John Rid and Androw Knolls, subtennents ther, and their wyves, poll is 1 4 0

Item, William Gibb, grassman, his generall poll is 0 6 0

Item, George Philp and George M'Allan, subtennents ther, and their wyfes, poll, 1 4 0

£6 16 8

WESTER CARNEY.

Alexander Smith, in Waster Karney, his proportione of the walowatione being 8s. 6d., with his owen and his wyfes generall poll is 1 6 0

Item, Gilbert Meney, servant, fee £10, the fortieth pairt, with the generall poll, 0 11 0

Item, Issobell Symson, servant, fee £6, the fortieth pairt and the generall poll, 0 9 0

Item, Gilbert Walker, servant, of fee £2, the fortieth pairt with generall poll is 0 7 0

Item, William Mannie, subtennent, his ovn and his wyfes generall poll is £0 12 0
Item, Robert Gallow, subtennent, his ovn and his wyfes generall poll is 0 12 0
Item, John Taitt, swbtennent, and his wyfe, of generall poll is 0 12 0
ARTHOUR MORRS, tennent, his proportione of his valowatione being 8s., with
    6s. of generall poll for himself and 6s. for his wife, is..................... 1 0 6
Item, William Sharp, his servant, fee £8, the fortieth pairt and generall poll is 0 9 0
Item, Thomas Shirres, subtennent, his ovn and his wyfes generall poll is.......... 0 12 0
Item, Alexander Wobster, subtennent, his ovn and his wyfes generall poll is ... 0 12 0
Item, Jo. Buren, subtennent and wywer ther, 6s. of poll for his trade, with
    6s. of generall poll for himself and 6s. for his wyfe, is.................... 0 18 0

                                   £7 15 0

A List of the Laerd of Skenes Tennents, with Valowation proportioned amongst them as foloweth, within the said pariochne of Skine, with his own and his [Ledy], and their Servants.

The walovatone of the Lands of Skein, belonging to the LAIRD of SKEINE,
    within the said pariochin, is £700 0 0

The hundreth pairt whereof, payable be the tennents, is............................. £7 0 0

Alexander Skein, of that ilk, is lyable in the poll of £12, he being above £500
    of valowation, and not exceeding £1000, with his oven and his ledys
    generall poll is... £12 12 0
Item, George Skein, his son, of poll is 1 16 0
Item, Thomas Skein, brother to the Leard of Skeine 0 6 0
Item, his two sisters, of generall poll is... 0 12 0
Item, John Silie, gardner, fee £20, fortieth pairt and generall poll 1 2 0
Item, Alexander Gallow, servant, fee £16, the fortieth pairt whereof and ge-
    nerall poll is.. 0 14 0
Item, Patrick Barklay, fee £12, the fortieth pairt and generall poll 0 12 0
Item, Alexander Silie, servant, fee £8, fortieth pairt and generall poll is 0 10 0
Item, Daved James, servant, fee £10, fortieth pairt and generall poll 0 11 0
Item, Andrew Lesslie, servant, fee £10, fortieth pairt and generall poll 0 11 0
Item, Elizabath Bannermane, servant. fee £2, fortieth pairt and generall poll... 0 16 0
Item, Isobell Findlay, servant, fee £12, fortieth pairt and generall poll 0 12 0
Item, Jane Gordone, servant, fee £9 6s. 8d., the fortieth pairt and generall poll, 0 10 8
Item, Margrat Snowie, the like fee and like generall poll is.......................... 0 10 8
Item, Agnes Gordon, servant, fee £6 13s. 4d., with the generall poll of 6s. is 0 9 2

                                   £22 4 6

The Laird of Skeines tennents, their proportion of the valowatione being in all, £7 0 0
    (Item, the Laird of Skein payes 9s. of walovatione, but not lyable, he being
        polled in ane heigher capacity.)
    William Creag, tennent ther, his proportione of the valowation, £0 9 0
    (The Laird of Skein, possessor of a pairt of the town and lands

of Haltone, but not lyabel aforsaid for 5s. 2d., he being clast
in a higher capacity.)

William Gordon, tennent in Hatton, his proportion of the valovatione is	£0	5	2	
James Miln ther, his proportione of the valowatione is	0	2	6	
James Grant ther, is	0	2	6	
(The Laird of Skeine, the town and lands of Bromhill, 10s., not layabel as aforsaid.)				
James Snowie, tennent in Leter, is	0	10	0	
James Smith, tennent ther, is	0	10	0	
William Thomson, tennent in Terevell, is	0	10	0	
Alexander Chessor ther, is	0	10	0	
James Edwart ther, is	0	6	0	
William Carneij, tennent in Affloch, is	0	6	0	
Alexander Edwart, tennent ther, is	0	6	0	
Robert Abell, tennent in Over Affloch, is	0	6	0	
Ronald Abell ther, his proportione is	0	6	0	
James Hall in Creagiedarg, is	0	10	0	
Androw Froster in Newtone, is	0	10	0	
			7	0	0

MAYNES.

William Creag, tennent ther, his proportione of his masters valowation is 9s., with his own and his wifes, and son *in familia,* their generall poll is	£1	7	0
James M'Petrie, servant, of fee £8, the fortieth part and generall poll is	0	10	0
Item, William Strayhen and Alexander Rae, subtennents, and their wives, poll	1	4	0
Item, Androw Lesly and Alexander Meney, subtennents, and their wives, poll,	1	4	0
Item, John Day, subtennent, and his wife, and Androw Day, his son *in familia,* their poll	0	18	0
Item, John Edwart ther, his generall poll is	0	6	0
	£5	9	0

HATTOWN.

William Gordon ther, his proportione of his masters valovatione is 5s. 2d., with his owen and his wifes generall poll	£0	17	2
Item, James Miln, and his wife, subtennents ther, of generall poll is, with his proportione of walovatione	0	14	6
Item, James Grant, his generall poll, with his proportione of valowatione, is	0	8	6
Item, William Scott, and his wife, subtennents, of generall poll	0	12	0
Item, James Lyon, smith, for his trade, for himself and his wife, generall poll,	0	18	0
Item, Alexander Hall and James Barron, subtennents, and their wyves, generall poll is	1	4	0
Item, Margrat Duncan, her generall poll	0	6	0
	£5	0	2

BROOMHILL.

John Watt, tradesman, and his wife, generall poll is	£0	18	0
Item, James Davedson and Daved James, and their wives, of generall poll	1	4	0
	£2	2	0

The parishes of
KINELLER and SKEIN
c1696

Note: Parts of Newhills, Dyce and Fintray
parishes were transferred to Kinellar 1948

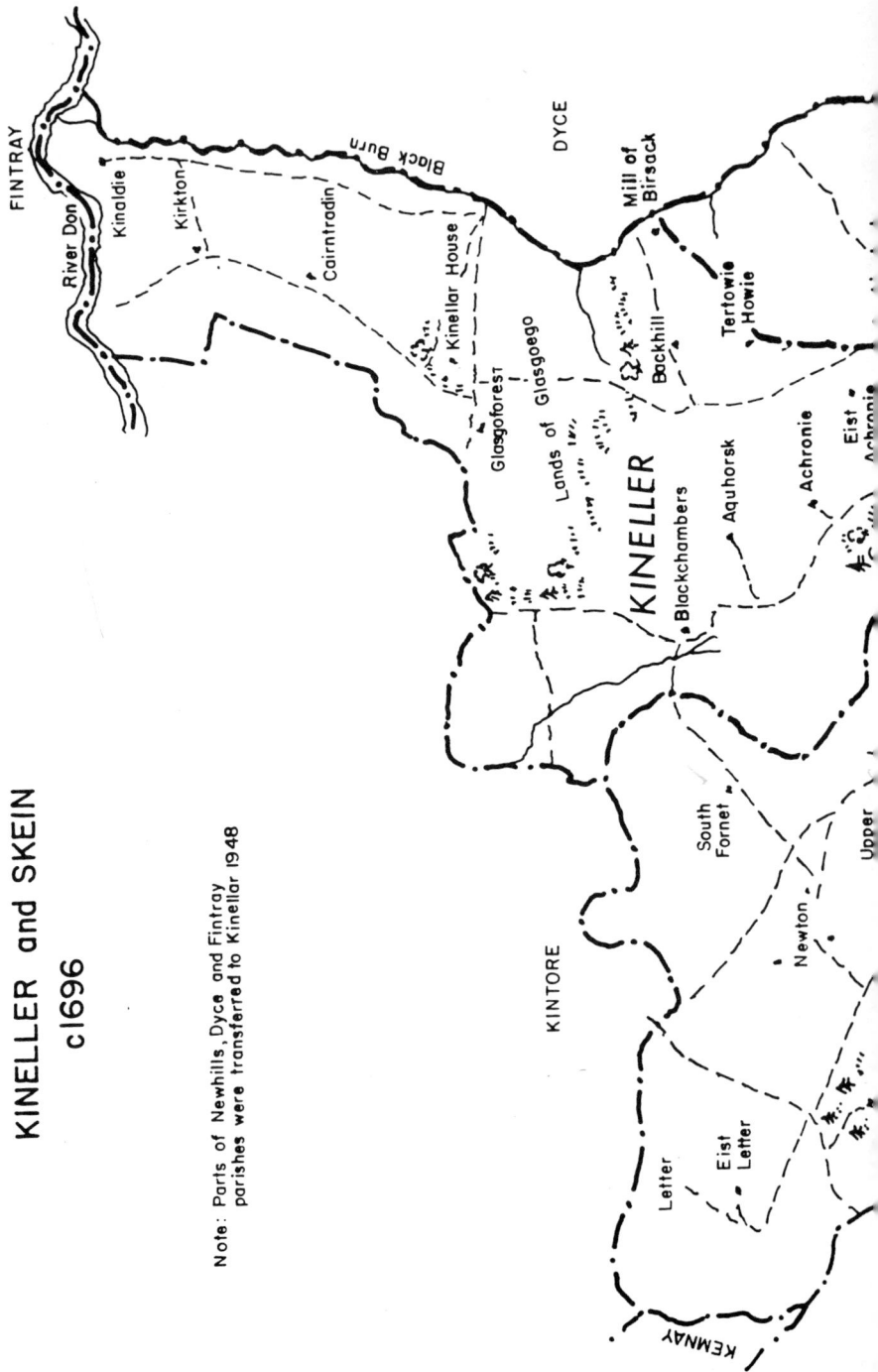

FINTRAY

River Don

Kinaldie

Kirkton

Cairntradin

Black Burn

Kinellar House

DYCE

Mill of
Birsack

Glasgoforest

Lands of Glasgoego

Tertowie
Howie

Backhill

KINELLER

Blackchambers

Aquhorsk

Achronie

Eist
Achronie

KINTORE

South
Fornet

Upper

Letter

Eist
Letter

Newton

KEMNAY

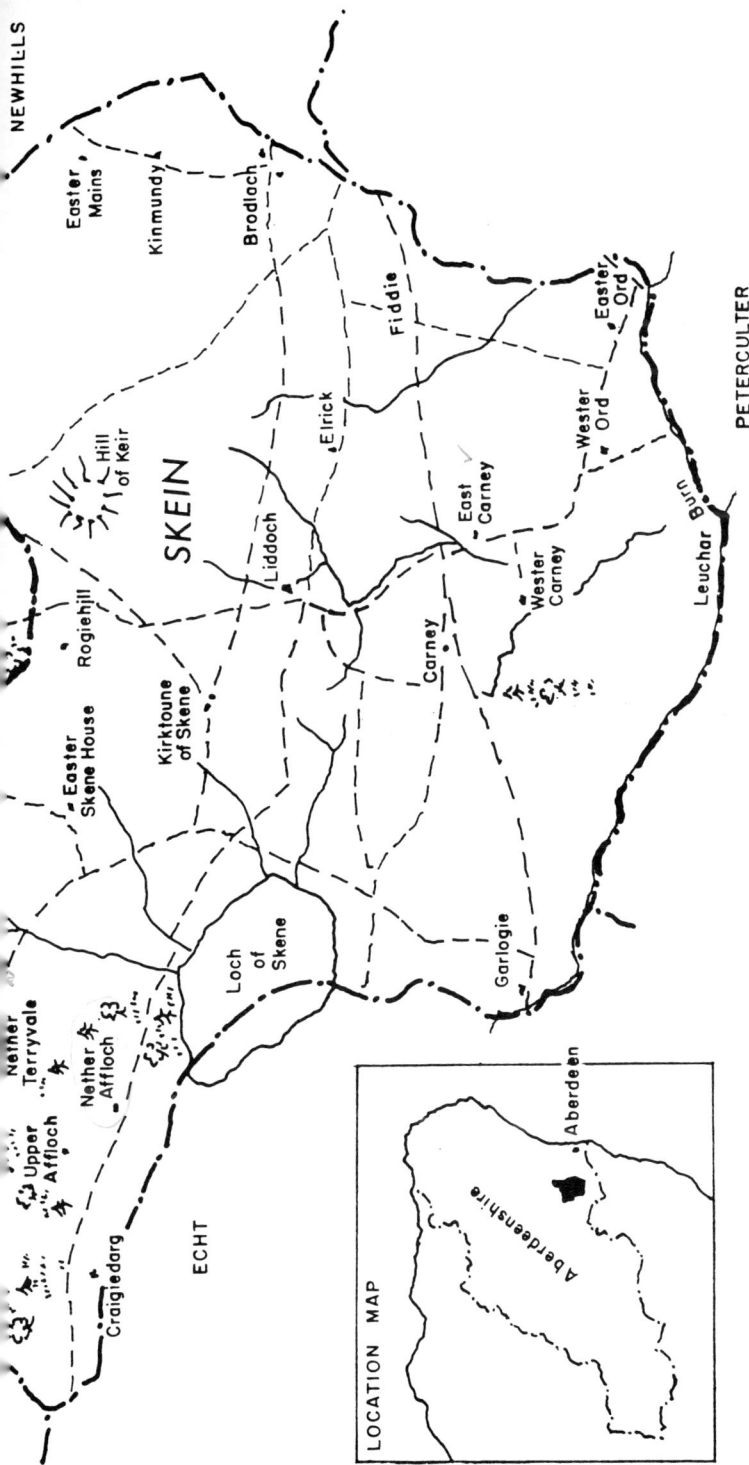

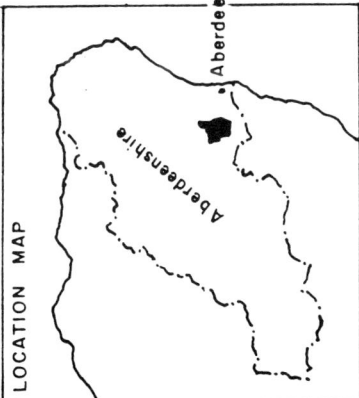

NEWHILLS

Easter Mains

Kinmundy

Brodloch

Fiddie

Easter Ord

PETERCULTER

Hill of Keir

Elrick

Wester Ord

SKEIN

Liddoch

East Carney

Wester Carney

Rogiehill

Carney

Leuchar Burn

Kirktoune of Skene

Easter Skene House

Loch of Skene

Garlogie

Nether Terryvale

Nether Affloch

Upper Affloch

ECHT

Craigiedarg

LOCATION MAP

Aberdeenshire

Aberdeen

NEWTTON.

Item, Androw Frost in Newtone of valowatione is 10s., with the generall poll
for himself, his wife, and William and James Frosts, his sones......... £1 14 0
Item, John Ritchie, Issobell Elderson, and Margrat Moir, subtennents, poll is, 0 18 0

£2 12 0

TEARAVELL.

Item, Wiliam Thomson, tennent ther, his proportion of the valowatione is 10s.,
with his oven and his wyfes generall poll..................................... £1 2 0
Item, James Gordon, his servant, of fee £10, the fortieth part with generall poll, 0 11 0
Item, William Smith, herd, of fee £2, the fortieth part and generall poll is 0 7 0
Item, James Crombi and James Watt subtennents, and their wyves, poll is...... 1 4 0
Item, James Strayhen, talzor, himself and his wyfe of generall poll is 0 18 0
Item, George Chesser, talor, and his wyfe and trade, of generall poll is........... 0 18 0
Item, Barbra Chessor, his daughter, generall poll...................................... 0 6 0
Item, Cristan Anderson, grasswoman, her generall poll is 0 6 0
ALEXANDER CHESSOR, tennent ther, his proportion of the valovation is 10s., with
his wyfe and daughter *in familia*, their generall poll is..................... 1 8 0
Item, James Hwnter, of fee £10, fortieth part whereof and his generall poll is... 0 11 0
Item, John Mill, of fee £3, the fortieth part whereof and generall poll is 0 7 6
Item, Alexander Forbes and Androw Meney, subtennents, and their wyves, poll, 1 4 0
Item, James Gillespie, smith ther, for his trade with his own and wyfes poll, 0 18 0
Item, Margrat Strayhen ther, her generall poll is...................................... 0 6 0
JAMES EDVART, tennent ther, his proportione of the valuatione is 10s., with
his own and his wyfes generall poll is 1 2 0
Item, William Brebner, servant, of fee £10, the fortieth part with generall poll, 0 11 0
Item, James Edwart, herd, fee £2, the fortieth part wherof and generall poll is 0 7 0
Item, Alexander Mourhead, servant, the lyk fee and generall poll 0 7 0
Item, John Skein, tradesman, for his trade 6s., with his own and wyfes poll...... 0 18 0
Item, William Meson, subtennent ther, his own and his wyfes generall poll is... 0 12 0
Item, Alexander Hervie, subtennent ther for his own generall poll 0 6 0
Item, Margrat John, grasswoman, for her own generall poll 0 6 0

£14 15 6

NETHER AFFLOCH.

William Kearney, tennent ther, the proportion of his masters walued rent, with
his own and his wyfes generall poll is..................................... 0 18 0
Item, Williame Alsiner, servant, of fee £12, the fortieth part and generall poll, 0 12 0
Item, Isobell Clark, servant, of fee £8, the fortieth part and generall poll is 0 10 0
Item, Alexander Gae, herd, of fee £2, the fortieth part and generall poll is 0 7 0
Item, John Wat, tradesman, for his trad, his own and his wyfes generall poll..... 0 18 0
Item, [   ] Edwart, subtennent ther and his wyfe, their generall poll is......... 0 12 0
Item, Adam Watt, tradesmane ther, for his trad, his own and wyfes poll is...... 0 18 0

£4 15 0

OVER AFFLOCH.

Robert Abell, tennent ther, his proportione of his masters walowaton is 6s., with
his own and his wifes generall poll is.. £0 18 0
Item, William Mill, his herd, £2 of fee per annum, and generall poll........... 0 7 0

Item, John Mackie, and James Ried, subtennents, and their wives, of poll...... £1 4 0
Item, Elspeth Forbes, grasswoman, for herself, generall poll......................... 0 6 0
RONALD ABELL, tennent ther, his proportion of the walowaton is 6s., [with]
    his ovn and wyfes generall poll is... 0 18 0
Item, Alexander Duncan, servant, of fee £12, fortieth part and generall poll is 0 12 0
Item, George Robertson, herd, of fee £2, fortieth pairt and generall poll is...... 0 7 0
Item, William Davedson, subtennent, and his wyfe, generall poll.................. 0 12 0

        £5 4 0

CRAIGDARG.

Item, James Hall, tennent ther, his proportion of the walowatone is 10s., with
    his own and wifes generall poll is... £1 2 0
Item, James, Villiam, and Janet Halls, their childring, generall poll............ 0 18 0
Item, Alexander Miln, herd, of fee £2, fortieth pairt and generall poll is......... 0 7 0
Item, Gilbert Mill, herd, of fee the lyk and generall poll............................. 0 7 0
Item, John Reid, tradesman, for his trade 6s., with his oven and wyfes poll is 0 18 0
Item, Alexander Watt, tradsman, for his trade 6s., with his own and his wifes
    generall poll is... 0 18 0
Item, Robert Mackie, elder, subtennent, his generall poll is...................... 0 4 0
Item, Robert Mackie, younger, his wife, and Issobell Bisset, grasswoman, poll, 0 18 0

        £5 14 0

LETTER.

Item, James Smith ther, his proportion of the walovatone is 10s., with his own,
    his wyfe, and tuo childring, their generall poll is.......................... £1 14 0
Item, James Smith ther, for his generall poll is..................................... 0 6 0
Item, Thomas Marr, servant, of fee £12, the fortieth part and generall poll is... 0 12 0
Item, Alexander Gordon, herd, of fee £3 6s. 8d., fortieth part and generall poll, 0 7 8
Item, Alexander Booth, tradesman, for his trade 6s., with his wifes and his own
    generall poll is... 0 18 0
Item, Elizabeth King, servant, of fee £8, the fortieth pairt and generall poll is 0 10 0
Item, Robert Bisset, tradesman, for his trade 6s., his ovne and his wifes poll is 0 18 0
Item, Margrat Fraser, servant, of fee £10, the fortieth pairt and generall poll is 0 11 0
Item, Agnes Brovn ther, her generall poll is....................................... 0 6 0
JAMES SNOWIE, tennent ther, his proportione of the valovatone is 10s., his ovn,
    and his wyfes generall poll is... 1 2 0
Item, John Dwff, servant, of fee per annum £12, fortieth part and generall poll, 0 12 0
Item, William Porter, servant, of fee £8, fortieth part and generall poll is....... 0 10 0
Item, George Broun, subtennent ther, for his own and his vyfes generall poll, 0 12 0
Item, James Smith, tradesman, for his trade 6s., and his oun and his wifes poll, 0 18 0
Item, Margrat Wiliamson, for her generall poll is.................................. 0 6 0
Item, John Shipeard, subtennent, and his wyfe, generall poll...................... 0 12 0

       £10 14 8

BERVIE.

Thomas Currie, in Bervie, and his wyfe, of generall poll is......................... £0 12 0
Item, William Thomson, his servant, fee £12, fortieth pairt and generall poll is 0 12 0

        £1 4 0

Mr. JOHN DUNLAP, minister, his poll and generall poll............................... £3 6 0

Item, Elizabeth Dowglas, his mother, is lyabell for the third of the deceast
    husbans poll, with her generall poll, is.. 1 6 0

Margrat Dowglas, wodsetter, being £72 of walovd rent, is lyable of £4 of poll,
    with the generall poll.. 4 6 0

Item, Thomas Burnet, his servant, fee £16, fortieth pairt and generall poll is... 0 14 0

Item, Mary Douglas, servant, fee 16 merks, fortieth pairt and generall poll is... 0 11 4

Item, Janet Mitchell, servant, fee £8, fortieth pairt and generall poll is........... 0 10 0

Item, Agnes Walker, servant, fee 8 merks, fortieth pairt and generall poll is.... 0 8 8

Item, Mr. John Symon ther, generall poll is.. 0 6 0

£11 8 0

Summa of SKEEN paroch amounts to two hundreth and eightie pund, four-
    teen shilling, and eight pennies.................................... £280 14 8

PAROCH OF SKENE

NAME (both sexes)	PAGES	NAME (both sexes)	PAGES
KING Elizabeth	500	MILLNE John	493
William	496	MILN Agnes	486
KINTOIR Earl of	486	Alexander	500
KITH Julian	495	Androw	493
		George	493
LEITH Alexander	496	James	498(2)
George	489,491	MILNE George	490
James	495	John	488,490
William	489,496	MITCHELL James	487
LESLY Androw	498	Janet	501
LESSLIE Andrew	497	MOIR Issobell	494
LOGGAN William	488	Margrat	499
LOUSON Androw	489	MORRIS Arthur	489
William	493	MORRS Arthour	497
LOUSONE Andrew	493	MOURHEAD Alexander	499
LOW Alexander	492,493	MURDO George	493
Elizabeth	490	Margrat	493
Isobell	493	William	489,493
Issebell	492	MUREY John	496
James	492	MURRAY Alexander	495
Marjorie	491		
Robert	491	NICOLL Alexander	489,494
LYG John	495	NORIE Alexander	489
LYON James	498	NORIJ William	489,496(2)
		NORRIE Alexander	495(2)
M'ALLAN George	496	John	493
M'PETRIE James	498	NOSE James	488
MACHRAY James	492		
MACKIE John	493,500	PETERSON Thomas	491
Margrat	495	PHILP Alexander	494
Robert	500(2)	George	496
MANNIE William	497	James	493
MARR Thomas	500	Margrat	493
MARRE Thomas	494	PHILPE Androw	492
MASONE John	490	PORTER William	500
MELVELL Alexander	488		
George	489,491	RAE Alexander	498
Thomas	491	John	490
MENEY Alexander	498	RANE James	489
Androw	499	RANEI John	491
Gilbert	496	RANEY Alexander	490
MENIE William	486	James	490
MESON William	499	REID Alaster	492
MILL George	489,495	Alexander	493,495
Gilbert	500	George	489,492
James	490	James	489,492,494
John	499	John	496,500
William	499	William	493
MILLN John	491	REIRY Alexander	489

OCCUPATIONS

cordoner	5	sivwright	1
cottar	10	smith	3
gardener	1	subtenant	92
grassman	3	tailor	6
grasswoman	12	tenant	62
herd	30	tradesman	10
laird	1	walker	1
miller	2	weaver	13
minister	1	wodsetter	1
servant	93	wright	1

MALES   113
FEMALES   92

TOTAL   205

ANE LIST of the POLLABLE PERSONES within the PARIOCHIN of KINELLER, taken up be the LAIRDS *of* KINALDIE *and* GLASGOEGO, *tuo Commissioners appointed for that effect, and be* Mr. ALEXANDER MILL, *Schoolmaster at the Kirk of Kineller, Clerk and Colector appointed be them for the said Pariochen.*

THE WALOVATIONE of the whole pariochen is £880 0 0

The LAIRD of KINALDIE his valuatione in the said pariochin is.................. £280 0 0

The hundreth pair⁺ wherof, payable be the tennents, is................................ £2 16 0

The said LAIRD of KINALDIE his valuatione being above two hundreth pounds,
    is layable for the poll of £9, and the generall poll for himself and his
    lady is.. £9 12 0
Item, Issobell Forbes, his nyce *in familia*, her poll is............................ 0 6 0
Item, Alexander Thomsone, his servant, fee £8, fortieth pairt and generall poll, 0 10 0
Item, Agnes Geddes, his servant, fee £4, fortieth pairt and generall poll is...... 0 8 0
                                        £10 16 0

The said Laird of Kinaldie, as possessor of some of the Lands,
    his proportione of the valued rent is............................... £0 10 0
Imprimis, James Reed, tennent in the Mayns of Kinaldie, his
    proportione of the valued rent is................................. 0 16 0
James Wilsone, tennent in Kirktoune of Kineller, his propor-
    tione is.. 0 10 0

Alexander Rae, tennent ther, his proportione is..................... £0 10 0
Alexander Moir, tennent ther, his proportione is..................... 0 10 0

                                                                                     2 16 0

MAYNS OF KINALDIE.

James Reed, tennent ther, his proportione of the valuèd rent is 16s., and the
    generall poll for himself and his wife... 1 8 0
Robert Bennet, his servant, fee £18, fortieth pairt and generall poll............... 0 15 0
William Reed, his servant, fee £15, fortieth pairt and generall poll............... 0 13 6
Item, Isobell Reed, his daughter, her poll is.. 0 6 0
John Lindsay, grassman ther, and Jean Shirres, his wife, their generall poll ... 0 12 0
John Molysone, grassman ther, and his wife, their poll is 0 12 0

                                                                                     £4 6 6

KIRKTOUNE OF KINELLER.

James Wilsone, tennent ther, his proportione of the valued rent is 10s., and the
    generall poll for himself and his wife is..................................... £1 2 0
John Thomsone, his servant, fee £8 per annum, fortieth pairt and generall
    poll is 0 10 0
Item, Agnes Wilson, his sister *in familia*, her poll is 0 6 0
Item, ALEXANDER RAE, tennent ther, his proportione of the valued rent is 10s.,
    and the generall poll for himself and his wife is 1 2 0
John Smith, his servant, his fee £3 per annum, fortieth pairt whereof and ge-
    nerall poll is.. 0 7 6
Jean Duncan, his servant, her fee £4, the fortieth pairt and generall poll is ... 0 8 0
John Ross, grassman ther, and his wife, their poll is 0 12 0
Item, ALEXANDER MOIRE, tennent ther, his proportione of the valued rent is
    10s., and the generall poll for himself and his wife, is.................... 1 2 0
Item, William Hay ther, his generall poll is... 0 6 0

                                                                                     £5 15 6

CAIRNTRADLAINE—(*Being mortyfied land.*)

George Walker, tennent ther, and his wife, their poll £0 12 0
Item, his son, Alexander Walker, and William Bisset, his goodsone *in familia*. 0 12 0
Alexander Mill, grassman, and his wife, their poll is..................................... 0 12 0
Andrew Milne, weaver ther, and his wife, their poll is..................................... 0 18 0
Item, WILLIAM BISSETT, tennent ther, and his wife, their poll is................... 0 12 0
Item, James and John Bissets, his sons *in familia*, their poll is 0 12 0
George Melvine, grassman ther, and his wife, their poll is............................. 0 12 0
Item, JAMES BLACKHALL, tennent ther, and his wife, their generall poll is...... 0 12 0
Alexander Taylor, his servant, fee £4, the fortieth pairt and generall poll is ... 0 8 0
William Lesly, weaver ther, and his wife, their poll is................................. 0 18 0
John Donald, grassman, and his wife, their poll is..................................... 0 12 0
William Bisset, shoemaker ther, and his wife, their poll is............................. 0 18 0
William Mill ther, and his wife, their poll is... 0 12 0
Item, Barbra Hervie, his good-daughter-in-law *in familia*, her generall poll is, 0 6 0
Alexander Hendersone ther, his generall poll is 0 6 0
Robert Able, his servant, fee £8, the fortieth pairt and generall poll is........... 0 10 0

                                                                                     £9 12 0

The valuatione of the Lands of Achronie and Tartouie, belonging to the LAIRD of CRAIGMYLL, is .... £200　0　0

The hundreth pairt whereof, payable be the tennents, is................................ £2　0　0
William Thomsone, tennent ther, his proportione of the valued rent
is... £0　11　4
Alexander Byres, tennent ther, his proportione .... 　0　5　8
John Leith, tennent ther, his proportione is........................... 　0　5　8
Alexander Ritchie, tennent ther, is .... 　0　8　4
Thomas Ronald ther, his proportione is............................... 　0　5　8
John Donald ther, his proportione is..................................... 　0　2　0
William Chessar ther, his proportione is .... 　0　1　4
　　　　　　　　　　　　　　　　　　　　　　　　　　　　　　　2　0　0

ACHRONIE.

William Thomsone, tennent ther, his proportione of the valued rent is 11s. 4d.,
and the generall poll for himselfe and his wyfe is...................................£1　3　4
Alexander Sharp, his servant, his fee £12, the fortieth part and generall poll is　0　12　0
Alexander Tayt, his servant, his fee £11, the fortieth part and generall poll is　0　11　6
Alexander Clinterty, his servant, his fee £3, the fortieth part and generall poll,　0　7　6
William Mill, smith ther, and his wife, poll is ....　0　18　0
William Skeen, weaver ther, his poll is...　0　12　0
John Murray, grassman ther, and his wife, poll is ....　0　12　0
William Chalmer and Agnes Robertson ther, their poll is ....　0　12　0
ALEXANDER BYRS, tennent ther, his proportione of the valued rent is 5s. 8d.,
and the generall poll for himselfe, and his wife, is.........................　0　17　8
William Duncan, his servant, his fee £5, fortieth part and generall poll is.......　0　8　6
Elspet Blackhall, his servant, her fee £6, the fortieth part and generall poll is　0　9　0
James Johnston and James Smith, grassmen ther, and their wives, poll.........　1　4　0
Elizabeth Boyne ther, her generall poll is..　0　6　0
JOHN LEITH, tennent ther, his proportione of the valued rent is 5s. 8d., and
the generall poll for himself and his wife, is.................................　0　17　8
Patrick Dounie, hi- servant, his fee £5, the fortieth pairt and generall poll is...　0　8　6
Isobell Petrie, his servant, her fee £2, the fortieth pairt and generall poll is....　0　7　0
Alexander Webster, grassman ther, and his wife, their poll is......................　0　12　0
Item, ALEXANDER RITCHIE, tennent ther, his proportione of the valued rent is
8s. 4d., and the generall poll is..　0　14　4
Elspet Smart, his servant, her fee £6, the fortieth pairt and generall poll is...　0　9　0
Peter Clinterty, grassman ther, and his wife, their poll is............................　0　12　0
Gilbert Skeen and John Ritchie, grassmen ther, and their wives, poll is..........　1　4　0
THOMAS RONALD, tennent ther, his proportione of the valued rent is 5s. 8d.,
and the generall poll for himselfe and his wife is...........................　0　17　8
Item, James, Alexander, and Helen Ronalds, his children, in familia, poll is...　0　18　0
JOHN DONALD, tennent ther, his proportione of the valued rent is 2s., and the
generall poll for himself and his wife is...　0　14　0
Item WILLIAM CHESSAR, tennent ther, his proportione of the valued rent is
1s. 4d., and the generall poll for himself and his wife is..................　0　13　4

James Douny ther, and Agnes Thomsone, his wife, their poll is...................... 0 12 0
Item, John and William Dounies, his sons *in familia*, their poll is.................. 0 12 0
Item, Janet Farquhar, his servant, fee £4, fortieth part and generall poll is...... 0 8 0
William Bisset, weaver ther, and his wife, their poll is................................. 0 18 0
Thomas Duncan, grassman ther, and his wife, poll is.................................. 0 12 0

$$£20 \quad 3 \quad 0$$

The valuatione of the Lands of Aqhuorsk, in the said pariochin, belonging to
Mr. GILBERT KEITH, is £133 6 8

The hundreth pairt whereof, payable by the tennents, is £1 6 8

AQHUORSK.

John Thomsone, tennent ther, his proportione of the valued rent is £1 6s. 8d.,
and the generall poll for himself and his wife is £1 18 8
James Cantly, his servant, his fee £12, fortieth pairt and generall poll is 0 12 0
John Logan, his servant, his fee £10, fortieth pairt and generall poll is 0 11 0
George Clerk and James Leith, his servants, their fee £2 each, fortieth pairt
generall poll is 0 14 0
Isobell Johnstone and Margrat Logan, his servants, their fee £4 each, fortieth
pairt and generall poll is 0 16 0
Item, William Bisset, weaver ther, and his wife, poll............ .... 0 18 0
Thomas Duncan, grassman ther, and his wife, their poll............................ 0 12 0
James Leith, tradesman ther, and his wife, poll is 0 18 0
Thomas Broun, weaver ther, and his wife, their poll is 0 18 0
John Hervie, his apprentice, his poll is 0 6 0
John Bisset, weaver ther, and his wife, their poll is................................. 0 18 0
James Priest and John Logan, elder, grassmen, and their wives, poll is 1 4 0
John Logan, younger, and Alexander Forbes, grassmen, and their wives, poll is 1 4 0

$$£11 \quad 9 \quad 8$$

The valuatione of the Lands of Blackchambers, in the said pariochin, belonging to Master THOMAS OREM, is... £133 6 8

The hundreth part whereof, payable by the tennents, is £1 6 8

The said Mr. Thomas Orem his valuatione in the said pariochin being above
fifty pound, is layable in the poll of £4, and the generall poll for him-
self and his wife is £4 12 0
Item, William Orem, his son *in familia*, his poll is..................................... 0 6 0
Alexander Walker, his servant, his fee £16, fortieth pairt and generall poll is... 0 14 0
Barbra Broune, his servant, her fee £8, the fortieth pairt and generall poll is... 0 10 0
Janet Mathewson, his servant, her fee £4, fortieth pairt and generall poll is... 0 8 0
ALEXANDER WOOD, tennent ther, his proportione of the valued rent and ge-
nerall poll for himself and his wife is 0 17 4
Andrew Edward, his servant, his fee £8, the fortieth pairt and generall poll.... 0 10 0

John Roy, his servant, fee £4, fortieth pairt and generall poll is £0 8 0
Isobell Logan, his servant, fee £5, fortieth pairt and generall poll is 0 8 6
Alexander Hunter and William Hunter, taylors ther, and their wife, their poll 1 16 0
Elspet Beaverly ther, her generall poll is... 0 6 0
George Robertsone, grassman ther, and his wife, their poll is....................... 0 12 0
Item, ROBERT HALL, tennent ther, his proportione of the valued rent and ge-
  nerall poll for himself, his wife, and Margrat Wood, his good-sister *in*
  familia, is 1 3 6
John Bisset, his servant, fee £10, fortieth pairt and generall poll is.............. 0 11 0
Alexander Mackallan, his servant, fee £4, fortieth pairt and generall poll is ... 0 8 0
William Broune, weaver ther, and his wife, their poll is 0 18 0
Alexander Deins, William Millne, and George Frost, grassmen ther, and their
  wives, their poll is 1 16 0

£16 4 4

The valuatione of the Lands of Glasgoego, in the said pariochin, belonging to
  JOHN KEITH, is..£133 6 8

The hundreth pairt whereof, payable by the tennents, is............................ £1 6 8

Mr. JOHN KEITH, tennent ther, his poll (he classing himselfe as ane gentle-
  man) is £3, and the generall poll for himselfe and his wife, their poll, £3 12 0
Robert Mill, his servant, his fee £10, fortieth pairt and generall poll is.......... 0 11 0
Issobell Mercer, his servant, fee £5, fortieth pairt and generall poll is............ 0 8 6
Janet Murray, servant, fee £5, fortieth pairt and generall poll is................... 0 8 6
John Smith, grassman ther, and his wife, their poll is.................................. 0 12 0
William Broune, weaver ther, and his wife, their poll is............................. 0 18 0
JAMES BISSET, tennent ther, his proportione of the valued rent, and the gene-
  rall poll for himself and his wife, is... 0 18 8
William Edwards, grassman ther, and his wife, their poll is........................ 0 12 0
Item, WILLIAM GRAY, tennent ther, his proportione of the valued rent is, and
  generall poll for himselfe and wife.. 0 18 8

£8 19 4

GLASGO FORREST.
GEORGE KELLIE, tennent ther, his proportion of the valued rent, and generall
  poll for himself and his wife.. £0 17 6
John Deans, his servant, fee £6, fortieth pairt and generall poll is................. 0 9 0
Margrat Menzies, his servant, fee £5, fortieth pairt and generall poll is........... 0 8 6
Alexander Robb, taylor ther, and his wife, their poll is............................ 0 18 0
William Andersone, wright ther, and his wife, their poll is......................... 0 18 0
George Ritchie, grassman ther, and his wife, poll is.................................... 0 12 0
Item, ANDREW GRAY, tennent ther, his proportione of the valued rent, and
  generall poll for himselfe and wife, is.. 0 17 4
Alexander Gray and Margrat Gray, his children *in familia,* their poll is......... 0 12 0
William Duff, weaver ther, and his wife and daughter, Elspet Duff, *in familia,*
  their poll is... 1 4 0

James Philip, tennent ther, his proportione of the valued rent, and generall
poll for himself, his wyfe, and son, John, *in familia*, is........................ £1 3 4
John Wagrell, grassman ther, and his wife, their poll.............................. 0 12 0

£8 11 8

Minister of Kineller.

Mr. George Smith, minister ther, his poll is... £3 6 0
Item, James Duncan, his servant, fee £8 6s. 8d., fortieth pairt and generall poll, 0 10 8
Jean George, his servant, fee £12, fortieth parit and generall poll is.............. 0 12 0
Marjorie Bisset, his servant, fee £4, fortieth pairt and generall poll is........... 0 8 0

£4 16 8

Summa of KINELLER paroch amounts to ane hundreth pund fourtein shilling
and eight pennies.. £100 14 8

PAROCH OF KINELLER

OCCUPATIONS

Clerk/Collector	1	Shoemaker	1
Grassman	27	Smith	1
Minister	1	Taylor	3
Schoolmaster	1	Weaver	9
Servants	40	Wright	1